"Steve Knox brings out tl [barcode: M000194757] want to leave a dent in th will help you do it. One of the best decisions of my career was hiring Steve for his mentorship in my personal and business life."

—Vince Gabriele, CEO of GFP and
Co-Founder of Million Dollar Gym.

"Gandhi famously said, 'Be the change you wish to see in the world.' Steve Knox lives this out with his expertise on leadership in a greater way than anyone I have known. His insight has empowered me personally and given ways to creatively seek solutions organizationally."

—Vernon Burger II, PhD,
Founder of His Voice Global

"Guru. Innovator. Brilliant. Witty. Sharp. Driven. This is Steve Knox. I've known Steve for nearly a decade and I can honestly say that with each encounter with him I've walked away a better version of myself. Steve has a way of seeing who you are and saying exactly what you need to hear (even if it's not what you want to hear). I am more confident, my marriage is healthier, and my business is thriving, thanks, in large part, to Steve."

—Becky Kiser, Sacred Holidays Founder
and Lead Writer

"I've participated in one of Steve Knox's Four Work Styles seminars and watched as our team came to life. He comes across as passionate, intelligent, and genuinely interested in helping teams work better together. Finally, a lot of his material is now in print in this brilliant book. Read it. Your team will benefit greatly from it."

—Michael Frost, Morling College, Sydney,
author, *The Shaping of Things to Come*

THE ASYMMETRICAL LEADER

Embrace Your Weaknesses.
Unleash Your Strengths.

STEVE KNOX

LUCIDBOOKS

The Asymmetrical Leader
Copyright © 2016 by Steve Knox

Published by Lucid Books in Houston, TX.
www.LucidBooks.net

First Printing 2016

ISBN 10: 1-63296-074-5
ISBN 13: 978-1-63296-074-0
eISBN 10: 1-63296-075-3
eISBN 13: 978-1-63296-075-7

Special Sales: Most Lucid Books titles are available in special quantity discounts. Custom imprinting or excerpting can also be done to fit special needs. Contact Lucid Books at info@lucidbooks.net.

A WORD BEFORE

ASYMMETRY IS A gift that every human being is born with. You might have spent your life up to this point interpreting your asymmetry as a weakness, limitation or deficit. You would be wrong. Dead wrong.

The truth is your asymmetry reveals your inner genius.

What you lack highlights what you have to offer.

Somewhere along the way someone told you to focus your time and attention fixing the very thing that makes you uniquely you.

This couldn't be further from the truth. They told you a lie.

You should acknowledge what you're not, and embrace all that you are.

Lean into your giftedness, your talent, your strength, your inner genius.

You will make your greatest contribution in life when you accept who you are and fully embrace the good, acknowledge the bad and play to your strengths.

There is no such thing as a whole person in this life.

You are broken in some beautiful way. In your brokenness you realize your need for others. Where you are weak, they are strong. Where you are gifted, others are lacking.

Genuine fulfillment will come when you discover your reason for being here—your unique gift to the world.

When you offer that gift—your true and best self—to others for a purpose bigger than yourself, you will experience genuine freedom, joy and life.

It's through giving yourself away that you become fully alive.

Overcoming the challenges in your life is not only possible, it is essential in creating the life you have been designed to live.

See your asymmetry for what it really is: a gift that makes you uniquely you.

There are 5 practices of asymmetry you can begin to cultivate in your daily life. These 5 practices will help you to develop a deeper awareness of who you are and the unique gift you have to offer the world.

Clarity: Why Are You Here?

Communication: What Is Your Story?

Collaboration: Who Do You Need?

Connection: What Is At Stake?

Cultivation: How Can You Help?

You already possess everything you need to live a generous, abundant and remarkable life.

You might want to reread that last sentence.

These are basic principles that you can apply today on your journey to creating the life you are meant to live.

25 CHAPTERS WRITTEN FOR YOU ABOUT:

CLARITY

Why Are You Here?

Practice 1: Clarity - Discover Your *Why*

Deep down you know what you really care about. You know what you're great at. You know what activities bring purpose, meaning and pleasure to your soul. You are a poem being written, a one-of-a-kind masterpiece being painted. You don't have to make a big deal out of your giftedness or draw attention to yourself; you simply need to develop your innate gifts, strengths and talent with all of your heart. As you acknowledge, embrace and pursue your best self, the sheer momentum of your life will open doors of possibility, opportunity and hope for others.

Chapter One

YOU

"Don't ask yourself what the world needs. Ask yourself what makes you come alive, and go do that; because what the world needs is people who have come alive."

—*Howard Thurman*

A SCENE IN the first season of Breaking Bad captures Walter White (played by Bryan Cranston) deconstructing the chemical makeup of the human body. His assistant lists all of the chemical components and comes to a final element missing from his biological equation: the human soul.

The ancients called the soul "the seat of emotions." The 20th Century ushered in a discipline of "soul study," psychology giving insight into the ego and the unconscious self. The soul is the truest and deepest part of you. It is who you are at your core. The soul is the full embodiment of your personality. It is what makes you, you.

There's a reason you are moved in what the Irish call "thin spaces"—heaven and earth being just a few feet apart, and even closer in certain moments. Birth and death. Marriage and divorce. Love and hate. These all touch us and affect us viscerally. They reveal our soul.

The bottom line is something bigger is going on here. You know there is. You feel there is.

If you want to make your greatest contribution in life, you have to live soulfully. You've got to do the hard work of discovering, developing and living from your highest and best self. Fulfillment in life comes when you discover and leverage your unique calling or gifting, when you put your soul into your work, your relationships, your life.

Self-awareness is key here. Self-awareness requires

clarity—in other words, vision. Literally translated, clarity means divine splendor. To live with clarity allows you to see the eternal worth and value you have to offer the world.

Clarity is about knowing *why* you're here. Understanding and embracing your unique self. Discovering who you are at your core. Uncovering those special gifts, strengths and talents that make you uniquely you.

Clarity is about acknowledging where you are weak, broken and lacking—and accepting these limitations, faults and deficiencies as gifts in disguise. It's through acceptance that your story is redeemed and can become a witness to others. A light in the darkness. A voice of hope for those in despair.

Clarity is about knowing when to listen and when to speak, when to take action and when to wait, when to risk and when to watch. This requires listening to your inner voice and developing the ability to be in step with your truest self—your soul.

Slow is fast here. To practice listening to your inner voice, slow your thoughts and work on mindfulness, being fully present to yourself so you can respond out of your best self. Gratitude is also key. Prayer works for some; journaling works for others. Finding what works for you is what matters most.

Defining your *why* is essential in living. *Why* is about purpose. *Why* is about meaning. *Why* is about soulful living.

Why determines how.

When you don't live from your core—your heart and your truest self—you end up frustrated, empty and apathetic. When you do, you become your best self.

What's going on in your heart? What wakes you up at night?

What dreams, passions or generative desires are rumbling around inside of you? Write a few thoughts down:

These are clues to your purpose—hints at your giftedness. Paying attention to them is vital in creating the life you are destined to live.

Think back to when you were a child. The world was full of possibility, curiosity and wonder. Somewhere along the way, though, your inner voice got drowned out by the voices of others. But real freedom is freedom from the opinion of others—especially when judgement creeps into your self-narrative. Judgment brings shame, which is emotional quicksand.

One of the first rites of passage into adulthood happens when you no longer reject yourself, when you fully embrace all of your story, both the triumphs and the tragedies, as a gift. Self-rejection is the biggest impediment to personal freedom and abundant life. Constantly questioning whether you are enough, whether you have what it takes, whether you can become the best version of yourself is a journey every human being faces. It requires real courage for you to accept yourself.

The ancient Hebrew word for this is *shalom*. *Shalom*, literally translated, means to "become whole, to be at peace within." One of the greatest gifts you can give yourself is to embrace both the good and the bad of your story. The faults and the strengths that have made you who you are.

How have your perceived weaknesses and faults been a gift in disguise? How have failure and hurt made you stronger and wiser? How can your brokenness be a source of strength for others? Write a few thoughts down:

These are all questions of the soul. Questions that call out your best self.

These questions reveal your *why*.

Being fully alive is about being in step with your asymmetry. Embracing your brokenness and realizing your full potential. If you want to change your life you have to own your story. You have to have clarity about *who* you are and *why* you're here. Your story is powerful. No one else has lived or can live your life. There is only one you.

Learning how to channel what you feel into real change will unleash your capacity for good in this life.

This is what it means to be inspired. To be in spirit. To live with clarity. To be connected with yourself and be more in touch with your purpose—your identity.

The good news is that you already have all that you need.

Chapter Two

VOCATION

"Discovering vocation does not mean scrambling
toward some prize just beyond my reach but
accepting the treasure of true self I already possess.
Vocation does not come from a voice out there
calling me to be something I am not. It comes from a
voice in here calling me to be the person I was born
to be, to fulfill the original selfhood given me
at birth by God."

—*Thomas Merton*

T HERE IS SOMETHING more, something greater in your life.

Your ability to tap into that source will enable you to live out your unique calling. Calling is the Latin translation of the word *vocation*. There is an idea, a dream that is calling you. It is unique to you.

You can find your calling simply by listening.

There are three hurdles you must overcome in order to live out your calling.

You must first redefine success. Success is a byproduct of faithfulness and consistency. Success is not about accumulation, but generosity. Success is an artificial way to define yourself. It is an extrinsic standard based on the expectations of others. Embracing your calling means tuning into your purpose and being faithful to create to your voice.

The second hurdle you have to overcome is the need to perform. Performance is not evil in and of itself—it's evil when competition becomes destructive relationally. Wanting to win no matter who you hurt or how much you damage your own soul is not worth it. Embracing your calling means tuning into your purpose and being faithful to cultivate your own voice.

The third hurdle is achievement. Achievement is a good thing when it's aligned with your calling. You are wired for progress. Your soul needs growth. Achievement becomes a stumbling block when obsession for perfection deteriorates your ability to connect with others in meaningful ways. Real achievement is living with integrity to your best and highest self. Achievement has more to do with compassion than it does conquering some massive goal. Achievement is about faithfulness to the present.

Who you are becoming far outweighs what you are accumulating. Spirit trumps stuff every time.

Your calling is built in part on your personality. You are wired a certain way. You have a preferred way of taking in information and making decisions that is unique to you. Through modern history and the study of human behavior, definable types of personalities have emerged. Psychologists and researchers like Jung, Birkman and Kiersey have all studied, written and championed this thought.

Through my own study of organizational and leadership psychology, I've renamed and reframed these into four leadership Work Styles™.

You can discover how you are wired to lead and live out your unique calling by answering two simple questions:

1. How do you prefer to plan?

2. How do you prefer to implement that plan?

Some people like to start planning by first considering the *details* of the project, task or new idea. Others like to start planning by first considering the *possibilities* of the project, task or new idea.

When it comes time to implement the plan, some people prefer to think through the *process* of accomplishing the project first. Others prefer to begin by considering the *people* involved in the project.

By looking at the combination of your preferences, you can figure out what kind of leader you are.

Here are The Four Work Styles™:

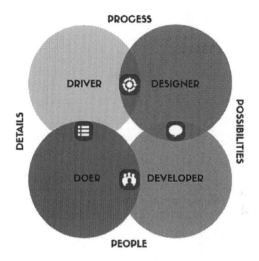

1. Details + Process = DRIVERS

Drivers are logistical leaders focused on efficiency, precision and getting the job done on time.

Drivers live by the mantra that "the leader is the lesson." They hold fast to the belief that the only thing that builds and sustains credibility is how they exemplify their standards of excellence and execution in real time. They literally drive behavior by focusing on the details of the process and striving for the most efficient way to operate.

- ▶ Drivers make up an estimated 35 percent of the population.
- ▶ Key characteristics: realistic, logical, pragmatic and systematic

2. Details + People = DOERS

Doers are tactical leaders focused on support, encouragement and getting the job done together.

Doers are motivated by the needs of others. They work diligently with a mental checklist of what needs to be accomplished in order to fulfill the commitments they have made. They literally do the heavy lifting and thankless jobs that most times go unnoticed but are critical for the task to be accomplished.

▶ Doers make up an estimated 35 percent of the population.

▶ Key characteristics: responsible, cooperative, tolerant and loyal

3. Possibilities + Process = DESIGNERS

Designers are strategic leaders focused on ingenuity, innovation and creating a better way to get the job done.

Designers are fascinated with what could be. They are motivated by the latest theory or strategy for getting work done. They desire competence in those they lead and those they are being led by. They literally design long-range solutions driven by curiosity and effective outcomes.

▶ Designers make up an estimated 15 percent of the population.

▶ Key characteristics: analytical, autonomous, clever and theoretical

4. Possibilities + People = DEVELOPERS

Developers are ideological leaders focused on engagement, development and adding value to the job.

Developers strive to live an integrated life. They are motivated by a deep sense of compassion and their own personal values. They desire inclusive work environments that are values-driven. They literally develop people, programs and products that will add value to the world today.

- ▶ Developers make up an estimated 15 percent of the population.
- ▶ Key characteristics: flexible, empathetic, original and enthusiastic

Chances are you may believe you are a combination of two or more of the Four Work Styles™.

Think of which one most aligns with who you are at your best.

You are the expert on you.

Chapter Three

POTENTIAL

"Your soul knows the geography of your destiny. Your soul alone has the map of your future, therefore you can trust this indirect, oblique side of yourself. If you do, it will take you where you need to go, but more important it will teach you a kindness of rhythm in your journey."

—*John O'Donohue*

W HAT FRUSTRATES YOU the most in life right now is a window into what you care the most about.

That frustration is a bright, flashing neon arrow pointing to the heart of the matter.

Which, of course, is your heart itself.

The only way to have a deeper sense of meaning and passion in your life is to tap into what you care most about.

Heart is about people. Heart is about values. Heart is about meaning and purpose and fulfillment. Busyness and the bottom line have crowded out your sense of calling—vocation. You heart is what will move you forward. Your heart is what gets you up out of bed in the morning. Your heart is what and whom you are fighting for.

When you reconnect with your heart—your purpose—you move beyond surface level existence and tap into what matters most—relationship. When you do this you gain clarity around who you are and where you're headed in life.

This takes courage.

Courage comes from the Latin *cor* meaning "heart." It takes real courage (heart) to change—to look deep inside at the inner values and passions that push you forward. Every human being needs courage to grow, progress and become fully alive.

The heart of the matter is the heart itself. In order to rediscover your passion for life, you have to remember every person you meet has a heart . . . they may just not be feeling or following it. What's in your heart? What are you most passionate about? Write a few thoughts down:

You have strength in you. You have power in you. You have greatness in you. You have inner genius.

Reread what you just wrote down. Think about how this list makes you unique. Acknowledge that these are gifts and talents you've been given.

Until the mid-14th century, the word *genius* meant "a guardian spirit," the belief that an individual's giftedness was the result of some kind of supernatural assistance or help. In the 17th century the word evolved to describe an individual with extraordinary and innate talent.

The etymology of *genius* is the word *to beget* or *produce*. In a real way, when you discover and develop your unique genius, you are living an inspired life. Living in spirit is about using your innate talent, abilities and strengths for the good of the world.

Your inner genius is a gift only you can develop.

The moment you begin to own your giftedness is the moment you take responsibility for your life. This is where fear kicks in. Feelings of self-pity, doubt and inadequacy stifle the pursuit of your truest self.

Self-pity is an emotion that can trap you. It's a cyclic obsession with self, where you become a victim of your circumstance rather than an owner and designer of a better life. Self-pity grabs hold of your ego and inflates every little negative word, experience or situation, distorting your view of reality. Self-pity is the opposite of acceptance.

The best way to overcome self-pity is to serve others. When you offer your genius as a gift to others, you shift your focus from what the world owes you to what you can contribute. This purposeful intention frees you from the sick cycle of self-pity.

Another trap is self-doubt. Understand that doubt is a natural part of life. Questioning your ability to rise to a challenge or overcome an obstacle is not bad in and of itself. Studies have been done that reinforce negative reasoning as a path to positive action, if and when you have performed a task before.

When you question your ability, you are tapping into past successes or failures. By doing so you summon the inner resources to the task at hand. But you cannot give into fear.

Fear is the opposite of faith.

Faith is choosing to believe today what will only make sense tomorrow. Faith is the spiritual word for trust. When you doubt you are choosing to not live in spirit. When you doubt you cripple your future.

There's a universal law at work here. When you do not use a gift you've been given, eventually you lose that gift. When you do not invest your time and talents, they waste away.

The best way to overcome doubt is to practice envisioning what your best self actually looks like. Positive framing gives you a clear picture of who your best self actually is. Imagine what your future self feels like, looks like, sounds like. Imagine what it will look like for you to be successful in what you're facing. Imagine what it will feel like when you conquer that fear. Write a few ideas here:

Feelings of inadequacy are negative patterns of thought learned over time. Somewhere along the way you began to believe a lie about yourself—that you were not good enough or smart enough or strong enough.

The truth is, even though you have faults, you already have everything you need to live an inspired and purposeful life. Within you is the raw material to live an extraordinary life. You already possess the intellect, strength and ability to impact and influence others in meaningful ways. You are enough.

Strength is an interesting concept. For the greater part of last century, so much of psychology was focused on the dysfunction within humanity. In the 1970s a new movement was born out of the knowledge that there is something right with the soul. Something beautiful. Something innate and good.

This field of Positive Psychology was first researched and written about by Maslow and Fromm, and has more recently been championed by the likes of the Gallup Organization, Martin Seligman and Marcus Buckingham. The driving idea behind this branch of psychology is that human beings can and should flourish.

The roots of Positive Psychology go back even further into the major faiths of the world and into the practice of ancient Greek philosophers Socrates and Plato. This thread throughout human history captures the innate genius every human being is born with.

This includes you.

It is not only possible for you to discover your strengths, it is necessary for you to use them to create a better life, a better world. Your voice is needed. Your contribution is essential.

Gallup defines strength as the combination of talent (innate genius), knowledge (extrinsic learning), skills (practiced abilities) and investment (time spent developing your talents). Strength is you at your best. Strength is your sweet spot. Strength is the raw material your future is made out of.

But the starting place is self-awareness.

Discovering those areas in your life where you operate at your best and developing them to your full potential is your main duty in life. You have only one job in life and that is to fully be yourself. The only person that can stop you is you.

As a child you had areas and talents that came naturally to you. Instinctual gifts. Think back on memories when certain activities came naturally to you. What types of tasks were these? Describe at least one memory here:

There are four clues to your areas of greatest potential that you undoubtedly experienced in the memory you described above: passion, retention, fulfillment and flow.

Passion is the electric feeling you get deep inside your heart that moves you to take action. Passion is an overwhelming sense of rightness. You have a built-in compass that points you in the direction you should go. Passion is more than affection for a cause or task, its an intrinsic drive toward mastery.

Retention is an indicator of strength that you have within yourself. When you discover an area of interest your ability to retain information almost becomes effortless. Your curiosity is piqued and your mind becomes a massive sponge. You literally tap into an insatiable state of learning.

Fulfillment is a conscious state of immense satisfaction. When you are leveraging your innate genius, you enter into a peak state where excellence is a natural byproduct of your thoughts, actions and behaviors. Fulfillment happens when you connect the dots with your best self and a challenge worth your full attention. Fulfillment is more than a feeling—it's a state of being marked by excellence.

Flow is a mental state of living when you are fully immersed in a moment of focused intentionality. Flow is when you are fully engaged and enjoying the activity you are performing. Flow happens when you get lost in the task at hand. You experience flow when you are operating out of your genius— in that moment you are fully you, fully alive.

Learning to operate out of your strengths will open a world of possibility and create momentum in your personal and professional life. Leveraging your giftedness is about living an inspired and extraordinary life.

When you have the courage to fully acknowledge, cultivate and live from your truest self—your innate genius—your life takes on an unstoppable quality.

Failure and setbacks will come your way. Change and heartache are inevitable. But, something amazing will happen around you. It will begin to seem as if the universe is suddenly for you.

You'll begin to dream dreams and achieve them. You'll be able to not only see a better future, but bring that vision into reality.

As the ancients would say, a bit of heaven will come to earth.

Chapter Four

THINKING

"You can have anything you want if you want it badly enough. You can be anything you want to be, do anything you set out to accomplish if you hold to that desire with singleness of purpose."

—*Abraham Lincoln*

Y OUR MIND IS more powerful than you know.

Science is beginning to prove what sages, poets and prophets have known throughout history—your thoughts matter.

An old Hebrew proverb states that as a man thinks in his heart, so he becomes.[1] Once you believe you are something that is what you become.

Being successful in life is about mindset. It's a choice about truly believing in your innate strengths, talents and abilities. When you change your thinking, you change your life.

Uncertainty, however, creates doubt.

When you're unclear about your purpose, you begin to lose sight of what is possible. You end up giving yourself over to anxiety, fear and reservations you have about the future. You get stuck in your old ways of thinking.

The key to changing your life is to change your mindset.

Choose to see opportunity where others see obstacles. Begin to choose faithfulness and discipline over laziness and apathy. Choose to live your life with passion and conviction day in and day out.

Ask yourself…

> Has your mindset affected your personal satisfaction with what you've achieved in life so far?

Circle one: Yes / No

➢ Do you have clarity when it comes to your purpose in life and in your career?

Circle one: Yes / No

➢ Are you confident about what your greatest strengths, gifts and talents are?

Circle one: Yes / No

➢ Do you believe you are capable of living to your fullest capacity and ability in the present moment?

Circle one: Yes / No

Your life, your career, and your current state of being are a perfect reflection of how you think about yourself.

The good news is that you can change. And there's nothing more powerful than a changed life.

Anxiety cripples you because you end up living in the future of "what if." What if you fail? What if you succeed? What if you miss out on something better? What if you lose? But projecting into the future with an anxious mindset quickly becomes a self-fulfilling prophecy. Fear of the future muddies your ability to see clearly in the moment.

The opposite of fear, however, is faith.

Faith in yourself. Faith in your giftedness. Faith in your calling. Faith in your capacity to become your best self.

Faith is closely akin to confidence, which in Latin means "to trust within." Confidence is different from arrogance. Confidence is rooted in humility. Confidence is an accurate view of your giftedness, ability and capacity for good.

Arrogance is a distorted, inflated view of yourself. That's why the ancient proverb says pride (arrogance) comes before a fall.[2]

Whether you believe you have the ability to become the highest version of yourself or not, you are absolutely right. You are only limited by your belief in yourself.

The greatest catalyst and greatest obstacle in your life is you. If you're frustrated in life, good. You have an opportunity to discover your passions.

If you believe your circumstances have left you stuck in life, good. You have an opportunity to change them.

If you have experienced failure recently, good. You have a chance to transform that experience into feedback.

Everything in life happens for a reason.

A powerful and humbling reality is that you have the ability to assign meaning to what happens to you. You have the innate ability to shape your self, your world, by the meaning you give to your circumstances, by the label you put on your experiences.

You alone have the power to be a victim or become a hero. You alone have the power to give yourself over to despair or to choose hope. You alone get to decide whether your best days are ahead of you or behind you. That is the power of your mind. The power of the narrative you choose to believe about yourself. The power of your thinking.

The only way to reach your full potential is to believe in yourself. You are a gift; your life can and should be a masterpiece. You were designed to be creative, generative, hopeful and courageous. The starting place is in the battlefield of your mind.

You will become what you focus on—what you give your conscious attention to—what you choose to believe about yourself.

Do not give your power over to others. Do not allow them to determine your potential, your capacity, your life. You do not need permission to live a remarkable and contagious life. It is your choice. It is up to you.

Beware of those who would try to talk you out of pursuing your calling. Fight against the haters, the dream stealers and those holding you back from becoming your best self. Remove them from your life.

Focus on what gives your life meaning and purpose. Remember what it is you are here to do. Tune out the distractions.

Forgive those who hurt you. Listen to your critics, take what they have to say to heart, meditate on it and use it as fuel to pursue your calling with all that you have in you.

Sometimes your critics can be your best teachers.

When you fail, reflect on what happened. Learn from it. Use it as feedback to help you navigate a better way forward. When you get discouraged, take heart. Every human being on the planet has lost heart at some point. In that moment return to your passion. Return to your calling.

Remember why you started this journey in the first place. Remember your reasons for changing. Think hard and long about what it is you've been called to. Focus on the life you want to live. Visualize the future you know you've been called to create.

Challenge the unknown. Face your fear by changing your focus. Fix your mind on your giftedness, your genius, your strength, your talent.

Take control of your mind.

Determine in your mind to live out your calling no matter what comes your way. Believe in what is possible for you.

Ideas will come when you focus on your calling. Challenge your thinking. Refine your plan. Tap into your inner creativity.

Concentrate on taking the next step to make your dream a reality.

Take that step. And the next one after that.

It all starts in connecting your heart and your mind. Meditate on the truth in your heart and in your mind. Live with a sense of urgency. Go to work on yourself.

Trust your gut. Trust the feelings in your heart. Believe in what you've seen.

Change your thinking and you will change your life.

Chapter Five

CALLING

"There are, it seems, two muses: the Muse of Inspiration, who gives us inarticulate visions and desires, and the Muse of Realization, who returns again and again to say 'It is yet more difficult than you thought.' This is the muse of form. It may be then that form serves us best when it works as an obstruction, to baffle us and deflect our intended course. It may be that when we no longer know what to do, we have come to our real work and when we no longer know which way to go, we have begun our real journey. The mind that is not baffled is not employed. The impeded stream is the one that sings."

—*Wendell Berry*

Y OU DO NOT need a title, degree or permission to be a leader. You are a leader. You already have all you need.

The first person you lead is you.

You will never lead the masses until you learn how to lead yourself. Leading yourself requires enormous strength. The good news is that you already have this power within you.

You can live life on a new level. You can live with discipline and passion. You have it in you to live a purposeful life of intention and clarity.

It is necessary for you to be courageous. It is necessary for you to face your fears. It is necessary for you to challenge yourself. It is necessary for you to rediscover your imagination. It is necessary for you to be present. It is necessary for you to be brutally honest with yourself.

Take full responsibility for your life. Let go of the past and embrace the present so you can mindfully create your future. You owe it to yourself to trust yourself.

Pay attention to your habits. Your rituals. Your routines. Stop wasting time. Stop pursuing entertainment. Stop consuming experiences. Start journaling. Start working. Start creating.

Reinvent your life. Reimagine your future. Reengage your calling.

Lead yourself. Commit to a routine. Start waking up early and starting when the day is quiet. Meditate on your goals.

Pray. Focus on what you need to do today. Make a list of what you must accomplish.

Take care of yourself physically. Get the sleep you need. Commit to eating healthy foods that will provide fuel for you to achieve your dream. Move. Exercise regularly. Walk and reflect on your choices. Walk and think about your goals. Walk and search your heart.

Lead yourself. Commit to being honest with yourself.

Your actions reveal what you truly believe. Match them up with your promises. Have integrity. Be the same inside and out. Trust yourself and be trustworthy. Use fewer words and listen more.

Let your life speak. Let your conversations be focused on others. Let your choices reflect your deepest convictions. Let your *yes* be *yes* and your *no* be *no*. Stop using the word *can't*. Remove it from your vocabulary. Say, "I will" or "I won't." Be resolute.

Lead yourself. Stop making excuses for your unhealthy patterns of living. Take a hard look at the behaviors shaping your life. Write down 3 habits you need to adopt in order to change:

Ask for insight from people you trust. Listen intently. Take to heart the wisdom these mentors are speaking into you. Put that wisdom to work in your life.

Your routines shape who you are and determine your

future. Changing your routines will change your life. Your learned behaviors can be overcome. You can make progress. You can change. But, it's up to you to lead you.

Deep down in your gut you know what you need to be doing and what you need to stop doing. Listen to your heart. Trust your conscience.

That still small voice is right 99.9% of the time.

COMMUNICATION

What Is Your Story?

Practice 2: Communication - Rewrite Your Story

Pay attention to the inner narrative you believe about who you are and what is possible in your life. You become what you meditate and focus on. Don't believe the lies that others tell you or you tell yourself. You have strength in you. You have talent in you. You have passion in you. You have the power to change your life by changing your thinking. You can create a better future, a future that you're designed to create by believing the best about yourself and your circumstance. Refuse to place blame, make excuses or get distracted. Rather take ownership of your life, be accountable for your choices, and feel the full responsibility and weight to leave your unique mark on the world.

Chapter Six

VALUES

"Your beliefs become your thoughts, Your thoughts become your words, Your words become your actions, Your actions become your habits, Your habits become your values, Your values become your destiny."

—*Mahatma Gandhi*

S EARCH YOUR HEART and define your values. Your values shape who you are. Your values give your life direction. Your values make your life simple. Your values give you clarity.

When you discover and articulate your values, you are defining what matters most to you. You are laying bare your non-negotiable beliefs. You are giving words to your passion. You are providing definitions for the rumblings of your soul and the deepest longings of your heart.

What are the 3 or 4 non-negotiable values that shape your choices? Write them down here:

The key is to begin to shape your life around these deeply held beliefs. Your values provide you with stability in an ever-changing world. Your core will become rock solid, and at the same time you will become more flexible and adaptable with the daily challenges you face.

Your values will guide you in evaluating your inner thought life. When you define your values, you become comfortable in your own skin. You know who you are, why you're here and what you're fighting for. You begin to care less about the opinions of others and surface-level conversations. You begin to see through.

Over time your values will become an unconscious internal guide. You will begin to navigate opportunities and relationships based on what truly matters. You will be able to quickly and clearly say *yes* and *no*. Where ambiguity once reigned, thoughtful resoluteness will arise.

Your values will guide you in your decision making. When your values align with a person or opportunity, you can honestly say *yes* with all your heart. You can know whether the present is right—good—for you.

When you live by your values, you can have confidence that you are right where you need to be in the universe at this moment. You can accept the present as a gift.

Your values act as an internal compass and filter for what is true and what is false. You can finally live with confidence. Living by your values makes your life simple. Simple doesn't mean easy, just less complicated.

Think about a time when your values didn't align with your circumstances. Write about that memory, the feeling and emotions, and your frustration:

Think back to the last frustrating circumstance you faced. Chances are, you made a decision or responded without thoughtful consideration. Your values were compromised or misaligned.

You shouldn't just listen to your heart. You should start acting on what you know. Trust your instincts.

Everything in your life has brought you to this moment.

Stop complaining and placing blame about what's happening outside of your control.

Start focusing on what you can control.

What you can influence.

What you value.

Chapter Seven

STORY

"We live in a world where bad stories are told, stories that teach us life doesn't mean anything and that humanity has no great purpose. It's a good calling, then, to speak a better story. How brightly a better story shines. How easily the world looks to it in wonder. How grateful we are to hear these stories, and how happy it makes us to repeat them."

—*Donald Miller*

ONE OF THE fastest ways to change your life is to change your inner narrative. Communication is not just an external dialogue; it's an internal monologue that is on replay in your mind.

There is a certain storyline you have subconsciously chosen to live by. You have chosen to see yourself in a certain light, and that thought pattern is shaping who you are and what you believe is possible in your life. It is shaping the words you speak to yourself.

Words matter. Words have power. Words are the expression of thoughts, feelings and deeply held beliefs. The words you use reveal what you truly believe about yourself and what you believe about others.

What is your inner narrative? Be specific:

Before you can change your future you have to change your thought life. You have to change the language you use to describe yourself to yourself.

➤ What conversation are you having in your thoughts?

➤ Is your mantra positive and optimistic, or is it negative and pessimistic?

➤ Do you have an accurate and hopeful picture of yourself? Circle one: Yes / No

You are not what other people say you are. You are not other people's perception of you. You are the expert on you.

Choose to believe in possibility. Choose to name your inner genius. Choose to hold on to the deepest truth of who you are.

Humility is key here. Not thinking too high (arrogance) or too low (self-pity) of yourself is the first step in changing your self-narrative. Have an accurate view of yourself.

Look beyond the person in the mirror. Search your heart.

➤ What lies are you choosing to believe about yourself? Be specific:

➤ How are your limiting beliefs holding you back? Be specific:

➤ How have people's opinions of you wreaked havoc on your soul? Be specific:

➤ How has fear crippled you? Be specific:

➤ How has doubt frozen you from taking action? Be specific:

You have the power to change your life by changing your story. This requires courage, discipline and perspective. Courage to change your inner narrative requires self-reflection. You have to do the hard work of accurately answering the four questions above with brutal honesty. There are no shortcuts.

All the major monotheistic religions believe the world was spoken into existence. You are a divine word being spoken into existence.

What words do you need to hear in order to believe in yourself? To exist? To grow? To change? To risk?

Make a list:

You are enough.

That's what it means to believe in yourself. To believe in the truth that is you. To believe in the possibility of you acting from your true self.

Chapter Eight
CHOICES

"The really important kind of freedom involves attention, and awareness, and discipline, and effort, and being able truly to care about other people and to sacrifice for them, over and over, in myriad petty little unsexy ways, every day."

—*David Foster Wallace*

THE MOMENT YOU choose to act on what you know in the deepest part of who you are is the moment you embrace your calling.

It all starts with a conscious decision to become.

To become whole. To become your true self. To become a voice of hope for others. To become who it is you've been created and called to be.

Decisions are the most spiritual and powerful actions in life.

Choosing to believe. Choosing to love. Choosing to hope. Choosing to serve. Choosing to create. Choosing to work.

You have the power to create a better life, one choice at a time. Every moment, your choices shape your future. These brief pockets of time are more powerful than you realize.

The latest scientific research has broken down the concept of a moment into 3 seconds. The simple math on this is that you could potentially make 21,000 choices a day, assuming you're awake two thirds of the day. Not all of these choices are conscious; in fact, most of them are habits you've formed over time.

Any given moment you can choose atrophy or growth. Generosity or greed. Joy or sadness. Community or isolation. Action or rest. Life or death.

What a powerful thought.

There is a significant reason why mindfulness is on the rise across the globe. You are a part of the busiest, most informed, overworked, overstimulated and overcommitted society in the history of the world.

Slowing down and being present is one of the greatest gifts you can give yourself and the people in your life.

Slowing down enables you to create margin in your life. Choosing to embrace these liminal spaces creates much needed time to reflect, think and be conscious of your internal state.

Mindful living is the only remedy for a busy soul.

You have a choice to either burn out or take time out.

Science and ancient wisdom agree here. Regularly taking time away from your work is good for your soul. When you choose to pull away, your mind has time to recharge and your creativity is increased. When you choose to step back and rest, your body is replenished and your spirit is renewed.

The byproduct of this type of intentionality is the development of a healthy rhythm of life.

You have to actively choose to engage in a pattern of living in order to have a specific outcome—consistent action coupled with conviction. You will become the disciplines you practice privately.

You will reap what you sow.

You will become your daily decisions.

People may call you lucky, but deep down you'll know the fruit of your life is the result of your dedication, hard work and sacrifice to create the future you've been called to.

Choose to act. Choose to work. Choose to dedicate yourself. Choose to give your best. Choose not to cut corners. Choose to practice excellence in private.

You are your choices.

Chapter Nine

ACTIONS

"Your pain is the breaking of the shell that encloses your understanding. . . . And could you keep your heart in wonder at the daily miracles of your life, your pain would not seem less wondrous than your joy."

—*Kahlil Gibran*

E VERYONE DEEP DOWN wants to live a remarkable life, but not everyone wants to do the hard work of living a disciplined life. You cannot be afraid to go after what you want in life. Condition your mind, commit your body, and dedicate your time to going to work on yourself.

Do not shrink back from challenges. Do not give in to fear. Do not let failure, heartache, a lack of resources, or the absence of support determine your success.

There is a universe of possibility alive inside your soul. The journey of discovering what you are capable of is a journey you must take if you hope to become all that you are capable of becoming. All growth happens at the edge of what you currently know.

Taking a hard look at yourself can be quite a fearful experience. Most people get busy, burnt out, distracted and escape just so they never have to do the hard work of facing their inner demons. You may be one of those people, but there's a better way forward.

You cannot let fear rule your heart. You must accept discipline as a way of life.

If you do not consciously take control of your life, someone else will. Why would you choose to give someone else control over your future? Do not let fear, apathy, laziness or complacency rule your heart.

Focus on your goals. Go to work on creating daily rituals

that will set you apart. Commit to action, to routines that will empower and enable you to succeed.

> ➤ What do you need to start doing right now? Jot down at least 3 ideas.

> ➤ What do you need to stop doing right now? Jot down at least 3 ideas.

> ➤ What do you need to continue doing right now? Jot down at least 3 ideas.

Embrace the old saying, "Early to bed and early to rise makes a man healthy, wealthy and wise." This kind of discipline is rare. This kind of truth is uncommon.

If you truly want to be exceptional, stop pretending and start acting on what you know you need to do in order to change and grow.

Living a disciplined life is also about receiving instruction. Be teachable. Soak up the knowledge of the greats who have gone before you. Immerse yourself in learning. Develop an insatiable curiosity for wisdom and truth. Make yourself do the necessary things.

This life is about relationships. Whom you surround yourself with is who you become. Choose your heroes wisely, because you will become like them. Choose your friends wisely as well, because their habits, language and behavior will become your own.

List your five closest relationships:

1.

2.

3.

4.

5.

How are they making you a better human being?

How are they holding you back?

Make room for generous, noble and faithful teachers in your life. Let go of relationships holding you back and stunting your growth. Choose to surround yourself with people who are stronger, smarter and more successful than you are. Learn from them. Listen to them. Watch how they live.

The only way to change and grow is to practice daily disciplines. To change your habits. Start small and build on success.

Deep down you want to be challenged. You want to give yourself to something greater, something purposeful, something saturated with meaning. Do not settle for less than your best.

When you settle for less than your best, you are self-sabotaging. When you make choices that aren't congruent with your values, you are self-sabotaging. When you fail to live with discipline and consistency, you are self-sabotaging.

Where are you self-sabotaging today? Be specific:

Physically -

Mentally -

Relationally -

Spiritually -

When you feel like quitting, take the next step. Stay. Do not run and hide. Dig deep. Press on. Bend, but do not break.

You alone can stop yourself. There is no one else to blame.

Believe. Commit. Act.

Chapter Ten

TRUTH

"Above all, don't lie to yourself. The man who lies to himself and listens to his own lie comes to a point that he cannot distinguish the truth within him, or around him, and so loses all respect for himself and for others. And having no respect he ceases to love."

—*Fyodor Dostoyevski*

A CTION INFORMS LANGUAGE. Language determines self-belief. Self-belief unleashes potential.

Your potential is determined by your self-belief. Your self-belief is built on the narrative you choose to focus on internally.

Remarkable people know this in their bones. You can be one of them.

Write your plan down. Put it in a journal. Commit it to memory. Revisit your goals daily. Let them fuel your choices.

Where do you want to be in three years? In three months? In three days? In three hours?

I'll quote my friend Pete here, who recently told me, "So many people overestimate what they can do in a year and underestimate what they can do in a lifetime."

By defining your goals you will inevitably gain clarity and direction. You will begin to connect the dots between where you are today and your true self.

➢ What are your top three personal goals? Write them down.

1.

2.

3.

➢ Why do you want to achieve these? Be brutally honest.

➢ How can you start working on them? List out at least four concrete steps for each goal.

Goal #1:

Action

Action

Action

Action

Goal #2:

Action

Action

Action

Action

Goal #3:

Action

Action

Action

Action

➤ What will you need to do to follow through on these goals? Be specific.

Goal #1:

Goal #2:

Goal #3:

➤ Who do you need to help you? Be accountable.

Goal #1 - Name(s)

Goal #2 - Name(s)

Goal #3 - Name(s)

➤ When will you achieve them by? Set a deadline. Deadlines are lifelines.

Deadline for Goal #1:

Deadline for Goal #2:

Deadline for Goal #3:

Do the same process for your professional goals. Keep them simple. Make them measurable.

➤ What are your top three Professional goals? Write them down.

1.

2.

3.

➤ Why do you want to achieve these? Be brutally honest.

➤ How can you start working on them? List out at least four concrete steps for each goal.

Goal #1:

Action

Action

Action

Action

Goal #2:

Action

Action

Action

Action

Goal #3:

Action

Action

Action

Action

➤ What will you need to do to follow through on these goals? Be specific.

Goal #1:

Goal #2:

Goal #3:

➤ Who do you need to help you? Be accountable.

   Goal #1 - Name(s)

   Goal #2 - Name(s)

   Goal #3 - Name(s)

➤ When will you achieve them by? Set a deadline. Deadlines are lifelines.

   Deadline for Goal #1:

   Deadline for Goal #2:

   Deadline for Goal #3:

Consistent action over time leads to remarkable success.

Daily discipline lays the foundation for a successful life. If yearly goals are too big for you to think about, focus on this quarter. If quarterly goals are too big for you think about, focus on this week. And if this week is too big to get your head around, focus on your three big goals for today.

The key is to start somewhere. To start now.

Plan your work. Work your plan.

If you miss a day. Start again. If you fail. Start again. If you get sidetracked. Start again.

Stop making excuses. Start acting. Come back to your reasons for wanting to change. Let your positive emotions fuel you.

Allow them to pull you into the future you know is possible.

COLLABORATION

Who Do You Need?

Practice 3: Collaboration - Ask for Help

Asking for help is not a sign of weakness, it's a sign of strength. When you ask for help you're embracing the soulful connections of vulnerability and humility. *Vulnerability* comes from the Latin word for wounded. The counterintuitive principle at work in the universe is that all healing comes through our shared humanity. You are clothed with strength when you offer your wounds to others. Wisdom is acquired by acknowledging your need for others. *Humility* comes from the Latin word for earth or dirt. Humility means you have both feet on the ground, acknowledging that you are a part of the human story and you have a role to play.

Chapter Eleven

FAITH

"The ragamuffin who sees his life as a voyage of discovery and runs the risk of failure has a better feel for faithfulness than the timid man who hides behind the law and never finds out who he is at all."

—*Brennan Manning*

TWO OF THE most important questions you can ask yourself are:

> ➤ Do I like myself?
> ➤ Am I trustworthy?

Both are byproducts of faithfulness. Faithful literally means to be full of faith. The definition of faithful is "accurate, reliable—true to the facts."

Being faithful starts with accurately aligning your life with your giftedness. It means you allow your outside to reflect your inside. You trust your gut and work to cultivate a life of integrity.

Faithfulness is what your soul is thirsting for. That is why excellence in ancient history was always in the context of relationship. Being faithful means you will help other people live at their highest and best self as well. Faithfulness is the *how* of excellence. It's attention and intention on your part with the people that have been entrusted to your care. This includes your relationship with yourself.

If you're struggling relationally, it is possibly because you are not being true to yourself. You may not even know yourself yet. How can you possibly hope to make friends, be a good partner or develop a significant relationship if you're walking around in the darkness of your own soul?

Become the person you are destined to be. Your relationships will flourish, because there is nothing more attractive than humble individuals comfortable in their own skin.

When you're faithful to yourself, your very life will also give people permission to do the same. You'll become an example of hope for others, and your life will be inspiring. Why? Because you will be living in spirit, true to yourself.

Asymmetry is a gift here. When you accept yourself—the good and the bad—the broken and the best parts take on equal value. In fact you begin to see your limitations and defects as the best way to relate to yourself and others in truth. Your asymmetry stops being something you hide from the world, but rather a way in which you have a shared humanity.

Liking yourself is a journey, but there's a fine line between arrogance and accurate self-knowledge. Humility is having a clear and truthful picture of who you actually are. Arrogance comes when you focus too much on yourself. The key to healthy self-knowledge is to be aware without becoming obsessed with self.

Your asymmetry reveals your strength, your talent, your innate genius. Because, when you come to terms with your own shortcomings, weaknesses and vulnerability, you understand your need for others and you begin to develop real compassion. When you identify what you're missing and where you're lacking, you also can easily see the greatness that is inside you.

You alone can determine whether this is used for evil or good in the universe. You alone get to choose whether to hide or be a light for others. You alone.

Being faithful to your calling requires the courage to reach out beyond yourself. It requires vulnerability. The ability to trust yourself in the face of possible rejection, heartache and loneliness. Pain, rejection and failure are just normal life happening to you.

People-pleasing is a trap. When you lack the ability to be comfortable in your own skin, you seek to entertain and make other people happy. This behavior feeds your inner need to be liked and accepted. It is built on a false promise that will leave you empty and resentful.

So many people have stated this truth in so many ways: a sure way to fail is to try to please everyone. The only way to be fulfilled is to be faithful. Full of faith. Trusting that you are enough. That you are okay.

Yes, you are broken, but this brokenness is a gift in disguise. It is your main duty in life to embrace your limitations and offer them as a transformative gift to others.

When you are faithful to yourself, you embrace the paradox of freedom and deep commitment. Inner freedom to be yourself and a deep commitment to be with and for others. You become an integral part of a story bigger than your own. But this starts with you knowing, owning and living your story.

Keeping faith has very little to do with religion. It has so much more to do with the way in which you see yourself and see the world.

You will begin to see yourself as you really are.

You will move beyond identifying yourself as less or more than others.

You will know your place, your story.

Chapter Twelve

ASKING

"When we honestly ask ourselves which person in our lives mean the most to us, we often find that it is those who, instead of giving advice, solutions, or cures, have chosen rather to share our pain and touch our wounds with a warm and tender hand. The friend who can be silent with us in a moment of despair or confusion, who can stay with us in an hour of grief and bereavement, who can tolerate not knowing, not curing, not healing and face with us the reality of our powerlessness, that is a friend who cares."

—*Henri Nouwen*

A SK FOR HELP. Don't be afraid to invite people to journey with you. Your reaching out is not a burden to your family and friends. It is an opportunity for them to use their own giftedness to help you.

When you ask for help, you're inviting people to be their best selves. That is what the heart of collaboration is all about. It is genuine friendship in a cause. Collaboration is the work of a community. Asymmetrical people relying on one another.

Fighting for one another.

Serving one another.

You need other people, and other people need you. In nature this is called *symbiosis*. Literally translated as "a living together." Your life is made possible by the lives of others, and you enrich the lives of other people. You belong. You are needed.

You may have doubted this due to some sort of rejection you faced in the past. That rejection wounded you at a deep soul level. That pain is real because it is connected to a lesser story than you are meant to live. In that sense it is a lie. It does not call out your best self. It is a limiting belief, a lie someone else spoke into your life.

Stop doubting and start living in the truth that there are no accidental people in the universe. Every single soul exists for a reason. Everyone you lock eyes with is of immense value. This includes you.

Everyone matters.

This thought will change you from the inside out. And it changes communities from the outside in.

Being inclusive is a sure sign you have experienced a sense of belonging. You know your own limitations. You know you need others. Once you start asking for help, people will come your way. Ideas will become reality. Positive change will happen. Your efforts will begin to multiply. You will be amazed at what you'll be able to do.

The starting place is to put yourself in a place where you have to act. Where you have to reach out. Asking for help moves you outside of your comfort zone. It breaks through apathy and personal complacency.

Once others are involved you will feel a positive pressure and depth of contribution you have never felt before. This shared sense of ownership will move you beyond what you think is possible.

Who do you need in your life right now? Make a list:

Who do you need to remove from your life? Make a list:

You have a sphere of influence that is only a short conversation away from helping you create what you know deep in you soul you've been put on earth here to do. Your courage will give them courage. Your vulnerability will give them permission to share their own story.

Don't wait for people to come to you. Go to them. Share your passion. Take action. The sheer momentum of your asking for help and taking positive action will begin to create a culture of courage.

Ask for help. Ask for feedback. Ask for wisdom. Ask for buy-in.

However, shake the dust off of your feet when people do not want to be involved. Don't hold grudges—simply move on and invest in those who share your passion.

The starting place is with your decisive action. Your commitment to your calling. Your passion for finding what you love and humbly offering it as a gift to the world.

Chapter Thirteen
LEARNING

"When we least expect it, life sets us a challenge to test our courage and willingness to change; at such a moment, there is no point in pretending that nothing has happened or in saying that we are not yet ready. The challenge will not wait. Life does not look back. A week is more than enough time for us to decide whether or not to accept our destiny."

—*Paulo Coelho*

YOU MAY NEED an older and wiser voice in your life. Someone to actively listen to you and guide you. Someone who knows the questions that can help you take action because they're a bit further down the road.

No one is an overnight success. There are weeks and months and years of hard work that made people who they are. Mastery is a byproduct of sacrifice, diligence and a lifetime of work.

Learning is built on trust, so surround yourself with the people who will be trustworthy. Remember, relationships that last are open, honest and vulnerable.

Right now you may be listening to voices operating out of a victim mentality. Voices that criticize, voices that complain, voices that tear down rather than build up. Stop listening to these voices. Remove them from your life. Stop allowing their words to shape your future.

It is better for you to lose ten friends who are apathetic and gain one who is achieving their dream. Living an uncommon life can be lonely, but eventually people will be drawn to you when you take action, when you begin to live out of your inner genius.

Seek out the counsel of those who can ask you the tough questions that matter most. Seek out people who can help you cultivate the raw talent you have within yourself. Seek out wisdom, no matter what it costs you.

Continue asking yourself what it is you truly want out of your life. You will quickly discover the answers are painful, uncomfortable and costly.

Asking a trusted advisor, coach or mentor to share from their experiences will fast track your own journey. Listen to their words. Take them to heart. Meditate on them. Filter them through you own experience. Go to work on living out of that truth.

Pay attention to their personal experiences. Learn from their mistakes. Pay attention to their professional setbacks. Understand where they messed up, change your approach and apply that truth.

Learn from their failures and their successes, because they have gained wisdom from those experiences. Let your guard down when wisdom reveals itself to you. Trust your heart and listen to your conscience when wisdom shows up. Soak up every ounce of what you experience.

Wisdom is the ability to live life skillfully. Wisdom comes through failure. Wisdom comes from those who have fallen down and gotten back up.

Be faithful in applying what you learn from others. Truth is old for a reason. It doesn't change. You change, however, when you discover and apply it.

Embrace childlike wonder when you learn. Let curiosity rule your heart. Ask questions. Listen and learn. Get excited about what you're experiencing. Let those positive emotions help you to change.

Be courageous in taking calculated risks. Real courage is not bull-headed; it's kindhearted and patient. Take heart.

Soak up wisdom. Read. Journal. Experiment.

Benefit from what you discover.

Let your desires for recognition, respect, fulfillment and satisfaction fuel you to continue learning, asking, and listening.

Chapter Fourteen

ACCOUNTABILITY

"Well, I always know what I want. And when you know what you want—you go toward it. Sometimes you go very fast, and sometimes only an inch a year. Perhaps you feel happier when you go fast. I don't know. I've forgotten the difference long ago, because it really doesn't matter, so long as you move."

—*Ayn Rand*

R EAL ACCOUNTABILITY IS not to someone else, but to your future self.

Real accountability is never based on the past.

Real accountability is based on the future you have been called to create.

Real accountability is not about your memory; it has much more to do with your imagination of who you need to become.

Progress and growth are birthed when you imagine a better future, when you look at where you want to go and embrace the possibility that exists within you. You know by now what it is you want to do. You know what it is you want to accomplish. You know what it is you've been called to create.

Write down a descriptive, emotional picture of your future self. What kind of person do you want to become? What kind of relationships do you want to have? What will you be doing? Be specific:

Notice the description you wrote down describes your future self, not your past. You will never fulfill the calling on your life by looking back, because continually looking back creates guilt. Guilt is obsession with the past. Guilt is baggage you no longer need to carry. Guilt is a lie you choose to believe. Guilt is refusing to let go of the past. Guilt is white-knuckling resentment, an inability to forgive.

Guilt comes from Old English meaning "sin, crime and failure." It is rooted in negativity.

It is time for you to let go of guilt. To live in the present. To embrace conviction. *Conviction* is rooted in a Latin word meaning, "to overcome." There is a huge difference in living a guilt-based life and living a life of conviction. You have to choose conviction. You have to embrace a mentality of overcoming. You have to surround yourself with people who live with conviction. People who live true lives based on their values.

Those people in your life who always define you according to your past are only holding you back from creating your future. Stop listening to them. Refuse to define yourself based on your past. Define yourself by who you're becoming. Overcome your circumstances. Overcome your past.

It takes courage to let things go. It takes courage to let go of past wounds. It takes courage to let go of hurt and anger. It takes courage to forgive.

Even if people have hurt you in the past, you are the only one holding yourself back. If you're constantly looking back, you'll never have a vision for the future. Stop wasting your time and energy on things you cannot change.

What negative memories and emotions do you need to let go of? Be specific:

Who do you need to forgive? Make a list:

Who do you need to ask forgiveness from? Make a list:

Be accountable. Make a decision to move on. Make a
decision to act. Make amends.

Step into the future you've been called to. Stop allowing
your past to determine the direction of your life.

Chapter Fifteen
COMMUNITY

"The glory of friendship is not the outstretched hand, not the kindly smile, nor the joy of companionship; it is the spiritual inspiration that comes to one when you discover that someone else believes in you and is willing to trust you with a friendship."

—*Ralph Waldo Emerson*

COLLABORATION IS ABOUT inviting people to journey with you. It is about being known.

You have to come out of hiding. You have to stop playing small. You have to put down the masks of insecurity, arrogance and your false self.

Being known means opening up. Being known means risking rejection. Being known means being kind.

Kindness opens up the possibility of friendship. *Kindness* is rooted in the word *kinship*—what you have in common with others. Your shared humanity. It's where you get the word *kindergarten*. Literally, "children's garden." As a child you knew how to share, how to collaborate, how to play with others.

Your purpose has to be rooted in love. Your goals, your aspirations, your future are determined by your ability to love yourself and love others. The greatest gift you can give those you love is the gift of becoming your best self. Your calling only makes sense in the context of community.

The world needs you to be you. Your friends need you to be your best self. Your family needs you to be your best self. The universe needs you to be your best self. When you are your best self, you give others hope and courage to be themselves.

You have to learn how to live a generous life. Start giving now. Generosity will turn your life upside down, and your heart inside out. This is a good thing.

When you live a generous life you are making a difference. When you show up and give, rather than take, you become a force for good in the world. When you live a generous life, it flies in the face of consumerism and the lie that stuff will fill the void in your life.

Generosity should become a way of life.

Selfishness and apathy are byproducts of a sick society. Greed is the human heart at its darkest. Don't fall into that trap. Money is not the goal. Adding value to people's lives is. Money will come when you add value. See it for what it is. Wealth is a means to serving humanity. It is not an indicator of your self worth.

Real wealth is generated when you move from a transactional mindset to a transformational one. A wealth of friendship, a wealth of community, a wealth of shared wisdom.

You have the ability to live a generative life. To use your gifts openly and freely. Start today.

Don't get trapped by measuring success based on what you've accumulated. Measure your life by what you have given away. By the quality and depth of your friendships. By what you have in common with those closest to you.

Write your definition of friendship here:

Living out your calling is the least selfish thing you can do. When you become your best self, you'll have so much more to give. You'll be able to give out of the overflow of what you've been given. You will be able to share out of the abundance of your life.

You'll discover that the more you give, the more you'll be entrusted with. Give early and give often. You'll be amazed at the opportunities that will come your way to use your giftedness.

Selfish people are afraid of losing what they have; generous people live in the knowledge that all of life is a gift. Gifts are meant to be given, shared.

You are a gift.

CONNECTION
What Is At Stake?

Practice 4: Connection - Stay the Course

Start with the end in mind and have a roadmap for getting there. You are your rituals, your daily habits, your moment-by-moment choices. Do the deep soul work of determining who it is you want to become and what your unique gift to the world actually is. Pursue your calling one day at a time. Faithfulness and consistency give birth to credibility and trust. Your daily routines and rituals will reap a harvest of impact and influence that will inevitably change your life.

Chapter Sixteen

ABUNDANCE

"None of us comes into the world fully formed. We would not know how to think, or walk, or speak, or behave as human beings unless we learned it from other human beings. We need other human beings in order to be human. I am because other people are."

—*Desmond Tutu*

MOST PEOPLE OPERATE out of one of two mindsets: a mindset of abundance or a mindset of scarcity.

A mindset of scarcity is limited. A mindset of abundance is unlimited.

A mindset of scarcity is fixed and unteachable. A mindset of abundance is open and curious.

A mindset of scarcity is fearful of change. A mindset of abundance is hopeful for growth.

A mindset of scarcity is ego-driven. A mindset of abundance is others-focused.

A mindset of scarcity is obsessed with the past. A mindset of abundance is calm and present.

In order to adopt a mindset of abundance you have to take ownership and responsibility and also focus on the good in your life—especially the relationships you have been entrusted with.

You are hardwired for community. You have been created for friendship. To belong. To practice empathy and compassion. To move away from shame and guilt and embrace the freedom to be yourself.

A mindset of abundance requires that you really see others. Recognize their giftedness. Be curious about what makes them tick. Find out what their inner genius is and help them begin to live out their innate calling.

A mindset of abundance moves you to look for what you

have in common with others. Focus on your shared humanity. Practice putting yourself in their shoes. See things from their perspective. Challenge your biases.

Befriend the people on the fringe. Listen to them. Learn from them. Serve them. Focus in on what you have to share with one another. Let the experience sink into your heart and change your thinking.

A mindset of abundance moves you to be in someone else's life. Share their struggle. Sit with them for awhile. Suspend judgement. Let go of your ego. Let go of your need for control. Walk with them in their shoes for more than a day. Allow your heart to feel what they feel. See what they see.

A mindset of abundance requires you to shut up and listen. Pay attention. Share your emotions. Be vulnerable. Turn your chair toward them. Listen to their story. Socialize. Empathize. Connect.

Fight the urge to fix the situation.

Focus your attention on them. Listen without answering. Value them. Affirm their genius. Practice lived empathy. Practice indiscriminate compassion. See the good in them. Nurture it.

Speak into them only when you are moved in your gut to do so. Be a voice of hope that calls out the best in them.

Empathy and compassion require imagination. Empathize with those you think are above you. Have compassion for those you once viewed as less than you. Connect with those whom you thought were too far gone.

Listen. Encourage. Challenge.

Cultivate a posture of openness. Step outside your normal pattern of thinking and feeling. Focus on others. Be present.

Who you are becoming far outweighs the pain you have to endure.

When you fall down, look up.

Your life will have attracted people that can help you get back on your feet.

See them.

Embrace the gift of friendship.

Sink roots with people who are alive. Sink roots with others who are on a mission to live out their unique calling. Sink roots with encouragers, positive people. Sink roots with those who are committed to something greater than themselves.

Be connected.

Take ownership of honoring your commitments. Show up early. Stay late. Be present the whole time. Fulfill your promises. Keep your word. Embody integrity.

All relationships are built on trust. Do not look at others for what they can give you. Honor their humanity by giving your best. Being your best. Seeing the best.

Move beyond shallow relationships. Move beyond negative people. Move beyond those who view themselves as helpless.

Refuse to be a victim.

Never think more of yourself or less of others.

Cultivate an inner awareness of what's really going on with people. Listen behind their words. Hear their hearts. See their giftedness. Value them by paying attention.

Give more than you take from them. Provide more than you're paid to do.

Go above and beyond the expectations of others. Add value in every way you can.

Surround yourself with people who care about excellence.

Pay attention to the pattern of their lives. Learn from them. Take those lessons to heart. Apply them in you own life.

Your life is a reflection of your standards. You are like those closest to you.

Stop being an enabler. Set boundaries for yourself.

Set standards that raise the bar on whom you allow into your sphere of influence. Guard this inner circle.

Embody your values. Live your life on a higher level.

Chapter Seventeen

CREDIBILITY

"Do something every day that you don't want to do; this is the golden rule for acquiring the habit of doing your duty without pain."

—*Mark Twain*

I N ORDER TO live your calling out and cultivate a life of real influence, you have to have credibility. Credibility is built on faithfulness and consistency over time. Showing up is base-line living.

You should do your part. If you truly want to live out your calling, you have to do even more. Be even more.

You are capable of so much more than what you are currently achieving.

If you genuinely want to live an extraordinary life, you have to name what it is you are fighting for. You must define the cause pulling you into the future of your dreams. You have to have direction.

Defining the fight is key in sustaining yourself through the winds of failure. You will be battered, bruised, rejected and ridiculed for pursuing your best self. You will. Know this and keep challenging yourself. No matter how many times you fall, fail or stumble, keep getting back up.

Keep your focus on what you're fighting for. Feel it. See it. Live it.

Keep coming back to the truth of your calling. To the idea that captured your heart. To the work you alone must do. Do not listen to the haters. Do not get distracted by the masses. Choose to live an uncommon life. Cultivate a capacity for faithfulness.

It is important for you to understand the direction of your

life. Your habits, your rituals, your routines all determine where you will end up. The hard truth is this: you have chosen to be right where you are today.

If you get defensive reading that last line, you are proving the point. Your pattern of thinking and living have led to this moment. If you do not like where you are at today, then change your habits, change your routines, change your vision of what is possible in your life.

Start with the end in mind. Take a deep look and begin to carefully consider what it will take to make your vision a reality.

What kind of person will you need to become in order to make your dream a reality? Be descriptive:

What skills, knowledge and experiences will you need to cultivate in order to make this happen? Be specific:

Who will you need in your life? Rewrite your list here:

Start envisioning your future self. Start acting on your first step. Set a timeframe, a deadline. Work toward it. Evaluate your progress. Measure your steps.

Let these objectives guide you. Keep it simple. Lay out a framework for the qualities, milestones and markers along the way.

Revisit this list. Revise this list. Rework this list.

Believe in yourself when others doubt you. Believe in yourself when others abandon you. Believe in yourself when others take advantage of you.

Do not settle for less than giving your all. Fight. Dig deep. Work hard. Get up early. Go to work on making your vision a reality.

Start living according to a higher standard. Choose excellence when you feel like average is enough. Strive to be better. Live better. Think better.

When you feel like you cannot go any further, remember your first love. Visualize the future that you've been called to create. Let it sink into your heart. Let it elevate your mind.

Have resolve. Be flexible but do not compromise. Be adaptable but do not sell yourself short. Bend but do not break.

Start small. Focus on small daily wins. Daily rituals. Adopt habits that will lead you to realizing your dream. Practice. Adapt. Learn. Grow.

Keep fighting. Fight the temptation to quit. Fight the temptation to stop. Fight the temptation to give up. Stay.

Remain focused. Remain committed. Remain passionate.

Focus on what you're fighting for. Hold onto it in your heart.

All leadership starts from within.

The impact and influence you have publicly is a direct result of who you are privately. Everything eventually comes out into the light of day.

Don't try to convince anyone with your words.

Let your actions speak.

Stop getting distracted from working on your goals. Stop pursuing anything that doesn't add value, momentum or progress in achieving your goals. Stop wasting time.

You've got lots of work to do. Be focused. Grind it out. Do the hard work now. Delay gratification.

Let your actions speak.

Stop creating obstacles for yourself. Stop being consumed by what other people are pursuing. Stop seeking out entertainment.

Get serious about your calling. Live in your truth. Embrace your identity. Be dedicated to your own path.

Let your actions speak.

Stop lying to yourself. Stop believing old ideas that haven't worked. Stop reliving the same old day.

See what good you can do today. Get unstuck. Feed your soul and mind. Rise above your circumstances. Stay curious.

Let your actions speak.

Stop making excuses. Stop contradicting yourself. Stop hurting others and hurting yourself.

Your future is waiting for you. Your best self is within reach. Boldly step into your calling.

Stay the course. Be faithful. Work consistently.

Chapter Eighteen
MOTIVES

"Nobody sees anybody truly but all through the flaws of their own egos. That is the way we all see . . . each other in life. Vanity, fear, desire, competition—all such distortions within our own egos—condition our vision of those in relation to us. Add to those distortions in our own egos, the corresponding distortions in the egos of others, and you see how cloudy the glass must become through which we look at each other. That's how it is in all living relationships except when there is that rare case of two people who love intensely enough to burn through all those layers of opacity and see each other's naked hearts."

—*Tennessee Williams*

THERE'S AN ANCIENT scripture stating that out of the overflow of the heart, the mouth speaks.[1]

Your words are shaped by the motives of your heart.

Words are merely surface-level indicators of deeply held beliefs. When you are squeezed, tested and pushed, the words that come into your mind and flow out of your mouth reveal where you are and who you really are.

Talk is cheap unless you live the life to back it up. Your actions are fueled by the convictions of your heart. Your motives.

Every time you choose to live from the core of who you are, you embrace your destiny. You flesh out what matters most.

Here are a few ideas to get you started on this path.

Meditate on truth. Devour it. Let it sink into your bones. Let it permeate your thoughts. Let it move you to take action.

When you wake up in the morning, start your day in the right state. Revisit your calling. Read your goals out loud. Determine your top priority for the day. Commit to a course of action.

Say a prayer of thanks for another day. Be grateful. Envision your day. Imagine your conversations. Picture what progress will look like for you today. Feel it. Meditate on it. Go to work.

Then, be present throughout your day. Be disciplined. When you're at work, work with all your heart. When you're at play, play with all your heart. When you're at rest, rest with all your heart.

Live without regret. Live intentionally.

Keep your commitments. Don't try. Do. To be committed means you will remain faithful to your course of action no matter how hard or difficult it may become.

Push through discomfort. Persevere through discouragement.

Time is a precious commodity. Don't waste your time on what doesn't matter, those things that distract you. Don't spend today recklessly. Invest your time.

The return on investing your time wisely is a changed and abundant life.

When you invest your time going to work on your calling, you will realize you are stronger and more capable than you know.

As you go throughout your day, be grateful. Cultivate an attitude of thankfulness. Gratitude frees you from the grip of self. Gratitude moves you to take continued and sustained action. Gratitude keeps you humble and generous.

What are you most grateful for today? Make a list:

As you go throughout your day, be disproportionate in how and where you invest your energy. Give yourself to the things that really matter. Stick to your goals. Stay faithful to the number one priority of your day.

Say no. No to distractions. No to energy stealers. No to entertainment. No to detours. No to delays. No to old patterns of thinking. No to anyone and anything which isn't going to help you achieve what it is you need to achieve today.

Say yes. Yes to commitment. Yes to effort. Yes to possibility. Yes to hard work. Yes to passion. Yes to fulfillment. Yes to delayed gratification. Yes to progress. Yes to your future.

Reflect at the end of your day. Examine yourself. Search your heart. Look at your motives. Align them with your values and your goals.

- ► Did you give your all?
- ► Work hard?
- ► Compromise?
- ► Get side-tracked?
- ► Make progress?
- ► Change?
- ► Grow?

Devote yourself to being better tomorrow. Remember that pain is temporary. Pain reminds you that you are alive. Feel it but don't dwell on it too long. Use it as guidance for the blank canvas of tomorrow.

Write down the things you're grateful for every day. Read them out loud. Let these thoughts fuel your actions.

If you don't remind yourself of your calling each and every day, you will lose sight of where you're headed.

Remind yourself daily about why you're alive. Why you're here. What you're committed to. Your reasons for working. Your motives.

Write them on your mirror. Write them in your journal. Write them on your heart.

Stay the course.

Chapter Nineteen

EXCELLENCE

"My meaning simply is, that whatever I have tried to do in life, I have tried with all my heart to do well; that whatever I have devoted myself to, I have devoted myself to completely; that in great aims and in small, I have always been thoroughly in earnest."

—*Charles Dickens*

A DOPT AN ATTITUDE of excellence.

Quietly and confidently be present to the work of your hands. Quietly and confidently listen to the people in front of you. Quietly and confidently work on your dream and flesh out your calling.

Do not imitate. You may have mimicked others in the past, but you are only limiting yourself. Find your own way. Definitely learn from others, but let what you produce carry your fingerprints. Let it be an overflow of your own imagination.

Do not copy. No matter what the so-called experts say. Do not dilute your voice. Speak what is yours. Shape what is yours. Craft what is yours.

Do not steal. Stealing is worse than quitting. When you steal other people's ideas, you are perpetuating emptiness. Falsehood. You end up only living a lie.

Innovate. Be inspired by greatness, but make it your own. Be inspired by the giftedness of others, but let what you produce be intrinsically linked to your heart. Let it be an expression of the good you have to offer the world.

Rediscover your imagination. Rekindle your childlike wonder. Reignite your passion for learning. No matter what you do, refuse to take shortcuts.

Invest your time cultivating your giftedness. Learn all you can. Develop the knowledge and skills to make your dream a reality.

Time is sacred. Do not procrastinate. Do not put off tomorrow what you're meant to work on today. Stop wasting time.

Value your time. Use it wisely. Make a plan for today. Be present. Be awake. Be creative.

Where are you wasting the most time? Be specific:

How can you change this pattern of behavior? Be specific:

Where should you invest your time today? Be specific:

Do not be afraid of failure. Fail early and fail often. Failure is feedback. Failure is part of the creative process. Failure will not define you. Failure will teach you. Failure will guide you. Failure will eventually lead you to finishing.

Failure is a sign you are trying. Keep failing. Keep working. Keep learning.

What past failure(s) have you allowed to define you? Be specific:

Stop defining yourself at your worst. See yourself at your best.

What would you like to be known for in the future? Be specific:

Reread what you just wrote and share it with someone you trust who can help you process through this information. If you feel like it's too personal, take some time to journal and reflect on why this is important for you personally and professionally.

Follow through. No matter how painful. Stay committed.

Do not be afraid of pain. Pain is a part of life. Trying to

avoid pain is like trying to avoid living. Pain and suffering are the stepping stones of faithfulness. Stop avoiding pain. Embrace it. Feel it. Be stronger from it.

Pain reminds you that you're alive. Keep moving forward regardless of the heartache.

Pain is temporary.

Where are you avoiding pain in your life today? Be specific:

When you get tired, keep going. When you hit the wall, keep working. Stick to your plan. Stay faithful. Be trustworthy.

If you cheat yourself in private, you will cheat others publicly. Do not cheat yourself. Do not rob yourself of your future.

How are you cheating yourself today? What is it costing you? Be specific:

Setbacks allow you to choose a new route. Welcome them when they come. Reevaluate and press on.

The universal law at work here is that you reap what you sow.

If you're negative in your thoughts and actions, the universe will send negativity back your way. If you're generous and kind, you'll reap generosity and kindness from others. The more you give, the more you'll be given. The more you take, the more will be taken from you.

Stop playing small. Let go of your limiting beliefs. Cultivate a life of growth and share what you learn with others.

Chapter Twenty

MEASURE

"Nothing in the world is worth having or worth doing unless it means effort, pain, difficulty. . . . I have never in my life envied a human being who led an easy life. I have envied a great many people who led difficult lives and led them well."

—*Theodore Roosevelt*

I N ORDER TO reach your full potential you have to track your progress.

Accountability means you measure your progress, track your growth and set meaningful goals. The word for accountability in Latin means "to reckon, compute or render account." Accountability moves you to a place of transparency, liability and responsibility.

If you want to be successful in designing a life of impact, you cannot go it alone. You must invite someone into your life who knows you and has a genuine investment in your personal development. Regardless of whether it's a friend, boss, mentor or coach, you must have someone you trust who can give you feedback and encouragement when you fall down, lose track or mess up.

Once you establish an accountability relationship with a person, decide to be honest with this person, no matter what. Every human being misses the mark, but if you hope to live life to the fullest, you need to own the positive and negative choices you make. All growth starts with the truth. You have to be honest with yourself and others, no matter what.

Share what your struggles are and what you're learning. When you share, don't lie. Don't hide. You are only cheating yourself.

Be fully honest. Feel the pain of disappointment. Feel the joy of achievement. When you speak from your present reality, you will grow.

You should also track your progress, physically, in a journal. There's something primal that happens when you put pen to paper. Journaling has been a practice of leaders throughout history. You will quickly see the benefit of writing down your goals and revisiting them daily.

Journaling will help improve your well-being. Writing your thoughts down on paper gives you an outlet to digest and examine the highs and lows of your life.

You'll be more focused on what you are trying to achieve. You'll be more positive because you'll be actively checking off your achievements. You'll also increase your ability to recall what matters most and what you need to do next.

Writing in a journal will improve the quality of your relationships and your ability to deliver on your promises. Journaling is an active personal history that allows you to revisit your former self. It's a place to record your story, reflect on your choices and change the direction of your life moving forward.

Keeping a journal of your commitments and goals not only helps you stay on top of your to-do lists, but it even provides you with the perspective to learn from your mistakes.

Journaling will also aid your thinking. Writing will give you perspective to revisit your pattern of thinking. This self-reflection is crucial, especially when it comes to your personal growth and improvement. Complex ideas become simple over time with focus and attention.

Commit to reviewing your goals. You cannot achieve what you do not measure. And the best way to measure is to be honest with yourself by physically putting down a picture of your future on paper and sharing it with someone you trust.

CULTIVATION
How Can You Help?

Practice 5: Cultivation - Fight for the Greater Good

Offer your giftedness to a cause bigger than you. The starting place is awareness and gratitude for what you've been entrusted with. Aligning your giftedness—your inner genius—with the giftedness of others creates a groundswell force of hope in the world. Never underestimate what you can achieve when you are connected with and fighting for something of real significance. Community will be a byproduct. You will realize that generous people are never poor and hopeful people are never defeated— they have the gift of friendship in dedication to a noble cause. When you step out in faith, others will be attracted to your courage, and likeminded folks will lock arms with you.

Chapter TwentyOne
GENEROSITY

"The most important kind of freedom is to be what you really are. You trade in your reality for a role. You trade in your sense for an act. You give up your ability to feel, and in exchange, put on a mask. There can't be any large-scale revolution until there's a personal revolution, on an individual level. It's got to happen inside first."

—*Jim Morrison*

WHEN YOU EMBRACE your calling, you create an amazing capacity for generosity.

When you become more, you have more to give away to others.

Your courage will help others live courageously.

Your willpower will be a catalyst for others.

Your decisiveness will provide direction for others in your life.

Your humility will cause others to look deeply within themselves.

Your faithfulness will create a culture of trust around you.

Your intentionality will empower others to live with purpose.

Do not underestimate the power of changing your life. Let your life be an example.

Keep believing in yourself. Keep fighting for others.

The best way to help people discover their own calling is to live yours out fully. Do not settle or lower your standards. Invest more in what you're doing.

When you raise your standards, you redefine excellence in the lives of those closest to you. Press beyond average. Refuse to settle. When you demand the best of yourself, you raise the collective standards of everyone in your sphere of influence.

You challenge the thinking of others by changing your own thoughts. You empower people to rise above their circumstances by continuously overcoming the obstacles in your own life.

The world needs you to be you. The world needs you to change. The world needs you to become more than you are today. The world needs your voice. The world needs your contribution.

You can make the world a better place. You can make a significant contribution to humankind.

Let your life be good news.

Be inclusive, your life will be good news to the outcasts.

Be hopeful, your life will be good news to the depressed.

Be generous, your life will be good news to the impoverished.

Be intelligent, your life will be good news to those without a voice.

Be encouraging, your life will be good news to those who stopped believing in themselves.

Be strong, your life will be good news to the weak.

Be courageous, your life will be good news to those who have lost heart.

Be faithful, your life will be good news to those who have given up.

Be passionate, your life will be good news to those in despair.

Be productive, your life will be good news to those who have yet to find their purpose.

Be creative, your life will be good news to those who have stopped using their imagination.

Be open, your life will be good news to those who have cut themselves off from others.

Be you, your life will be good news.

Let your passion overflow in everything you do. Serve others.

How can your life be good news to those closest to you? Write down specific ways:

Chapter TwentyTwo

HAPPINESS

"Though much is taken, much abides; and though
We are not now that strength which in old days
Moved earth and heaven, that which we are, we are;
One equal temper of heroic hearts,
Made weak by time and fate, but strong in will
To strive, to seek, to find, and not to yield."

—*Alfred Lord Tennyson*

H APPINESS HAS MORE to do with your capacity to give than it does with your circumstances.

Happiness is a mindset. It's being content with what you have and holding everything you've been given with an open hand.

Recognize the seasonality of life. Every night has a day. Every winter has a spring. There is a time to sow and a time to reap. When it's time to sow, sow with all your heart. Work hard. Do the difficult things.

The only thing that will genuinely satisfy the longing in your soul is continuous improvement. When you grow you have more in your life to give away.

Happiness will overwhelm you when you work with all of your strength.

Happiness will flood your thoughts when you change your mindset.

Happiness will saturate your relationships when you live from your soul.

Happiness will permeate your life when you follow your heart.

You can be happy when challenges come, because you'll know they bring out your best.

You can be happy when failure comes, because you'll know it is a stepping stone to growth and progress.

You can be happy when setbacks come, because you'll know a new path forward will eventually emerge.

Your life will be marked by acceptance. Your faith won't shrink when tragedy strikes. Your focus will sharpen when the storms of life come your way. Your convictions will be strengthened in the face of overwhelming difficulty.

Know that life is seasonal.

The heartache and hardship you are facing today will soon pass.

Know that life is cyclical.

Every down has an up; every setback has a way forward.

The key to growth and progress is to remain hopeful in the darkness. Diligent in the down times. To keep practicing, working, striving, focused no matter what's gone down.

Happiness is not determined by what you have. Happiness is a byproduct of who you become.

When your work is aligned with your values, you'll experience happiness.

When your life is lived for something greater than yourself, you'll experience happiness.

When you move beyond focusing on yourself and connect in meaningful ways with others, you'll experience happiness.

You're ability to fully experience happiness is a direct result of your ability to cultivate meaningful and lasting relationships.

When you choose to fight with others for a cause you genuinely believe in, you will experience purpose and passion for life. You will also be happy as a result.

What about you? Who are you fighting for? Be specific:

Who is fighting for you? Be specific:

The best way to experience happiness is to do the hard work of being a good friend. Practice empathy and compassion. Serve others. Build a network of companions who share in your struggle, who are invested in your success.

Continue to reach out. All meaningful relationships take work.

Nine times out of ten you'll have to initiate. You'll have to be the one to step up. You'll have to be the one to connect.

Loneliness is hell on earth. Isolation is a sure sign of a sick soul. Hurting people hurt others.

You cure the disease of loneliness by offering your best self to the world. You cure the disease of loneliness by inviting people to journey with you. You cure the disease of loneliness by helping others discover their own path, their greatness, their calling—what it is that makes them come alive.

You cannot change people. You'll go mad trying.

People are changed from the inside out. Your life can impact and influence them, but it's up to them to change themselves.

Stay true to your calling. Stay passionate about the cause you're fighting for. Stay committed to executing your plan.

Others will take notice. Others will join you.

Be open. Be ready. Be willing.

Chapter TwentyThree

VISION

"There are two basic motivating forces: fear and love. When we are afraid, we pull back from life. When we are in love, we open to all that life has to offer with passion, excitement, and acceptance. We need to learn to love ourselves first, in all our glory and our imperfections. If we cannot love ourselves, we cannot fully open to our ability to love others or our potential to create. Evolution and all hopes for a better world rest in the fearlessness and open-hearted vision of people who embrace life."

—*John Lennon*

Y OUR ABILITY TO create a better future is directly related to your ability to have vision. To see more in yourself and articulate the possibility of a better future for others.

This life is about relationships. Vision empowers you to see the good in others and to help them see their asymmetry as a gift. This requires vulnerability and courage, sensitivity and intentionality.

There's an ancient scripture stating that without vision people perish.[1] Vision is more than a picture of a better future. Vision is a magnet that pulls you into a better life.

Most people you'll meet are stuck in life. When you begin to grow, change, experience success, people will try to hold you back.

People do not like to be left behind. The masses want to be validated. Your playing small helps them feel good about themselves. Their fear will reach out and grab a hold of you if you're not careful.

Do not be afraid to break free from the herd. Do not be afraid to risk rejection.

When you believe in yourself, when you act on your gut feeling, your friendships will change. You'll quickly see who is really for you and who is not.

Your ability to forgive others will determine your capacity to live a bigger life. Forgiveness and freedom are closely linked.

Not everyone will see what you see. Not everyone will believe what you believe about yourself. Not everyone will buy into your vision.

This is a good thing.

People will doubt you. Do not let their opinions of you shape who you're becoming.

People will question your motives. Do not let their insecurity shake your convictions.

People will attack you. Do not let their negativity and selfishness hold you back from pursuing your calling.

Popularity is not a sign of success. It's actually the opposite. Be careful if crowds surround you. There's a good reason it's called "critical mass"—the masses will eventually become critical of you.

Look for the faithful few. Invest in them.

Your life will be a force for good. Your passion will be a catalyst in their lives.

Do not wait for validation. Do not test the waters with trepidation. Do not hesitate when opportunity presents itself. Do not shrink back from big challenges.

Live a principled life. Work diligently on your dream. Execute your plan. Be grateful when others join you.

People come in and out of your life for a reason. Some to teach you. Some to question you. Some to inspire and encourage you. Some to test you. Some to love you. Some to challenge you. Be grateful. Everyone matters.

Every single person you meet has immense worth and tremendous value. Every person you lock eyes with has potential. They may just not see it yet. They may not have a vision of who they are destined to become.

The real gift of friendship happens when you're on a

journey to becoming your best self and you cross paths with someone else on a similar journey.

This is where genuine community happens.

Friendship in a cause.

Pay attention. Be present. Be a voice of hope in their lives. Give them eyes to see. Speak to their hearts so that they might understand and know how valuable and unique they really are. Help them own their asymmetry.

You have the capacity, the ability to expand their view of what is possible in this life. Do not underestimate your influence on them or theirs on you.

See the good. Reserve judgement. Suspend your ego. Fight the need to compete and compare.

Ask yourself who in your life today is making you a better human being? Make a list:

See the good in them. Recognize the good in yourself. Build on that truth. Cultivate a life of gratitude and thankfulness.

Your vision of the future must include people who care and people you are caring for. Life is empty without meaningful relationships.

Move toward community. Toward creating a better world for future generations.

Become more.

More loving.

More patient.

More open.

More giving.

More caring.

More joyful.

More human.

More you.

Chapter TwentyFour

MISSION

"Love is the only way to grasp another human being in the innermost core of his personality. No one can become fully aware of the very essence of another human being unless he loves him. By his love he is enabled to see the essential traits and features in the beloved person; and even more, he sees that which is potential in him, which is not yet actualized but yet ought to be actualized. Furthermore, by his love, the loving person enables the beloved person to actualize these potentialities. By making him aware of what he can be and of what he should become, he makes these potentialities come true."

—*Viktor Frankl*

YOUR MISSION IS your purpose. Mission is your *why*. Mission is built on the raw materials of your innate gifts, strengths and asymmetry.

Mission is the active expression of the belief that every human being on the planet is destined for something more.

Significance is a byproduct of understanding and living out your personal mission. Significance is knowing you have given your all in pursuit of your best self.

That your life has mattered.

That you have left your mark on the world.

That you have made your unique contribution in this one life you've been given.

That you have, are and will live out your *why*—your mission, your calling.

To live out your calling, you need other people. More importantly, other people need you.

They need you to rise above your circumstance. They need you to step up and stand out. They need you to lead. They need you to be your best self.

The way forward is to create community wherever you go.

Meals shared with those you love.

A job well done.

A smile.

The gift of friendship.

A promise fulfilled.

Giving more than you take.

Presence.

The moment you chose to become more for others.

You're probably asking, "Yes, but how?"

You have to be willing to reinvent yourself. You have to be willing to challenge your old way of thinking. You have to be willing to push beyond the status quo. You have to be willing to see potential and help it flourish wherever you might find it. Remember the first person you lead is you.

Mine your life for stories. Exegete the learned wisdom from your failures and your successes. Offer them as an example and warning to others. Share your defeats and your victories. Be open. Be honest. Be real.

Let your life be a compass for the possibility of soulful living.

Let your story motivate and move people.

Speak to the heart poetically. See with soulful eyes. Look beyond the surface. Listen for peoples hearts, their passions.

You'll quickly learn it is okay to be a bit of a prophet. In fact, it's necessary.

Call people back to their asymmetry. Challenge them to tap into their innate gifts, talents and strengths. Help them see their lives as a gift, their limitations as a source of hope for others.

Encourage them when they fail. Journey with them and help them cultivate an attitude and mindset of hope.

Let your words be in the right time and in the right tone. Not wasted.

Be present with people. Be with them. Stand with them. Weep with them. Celebrate with them.

Do not try to fix them. You cannot.

Set clear boundaries and high standards. Keep demanding more of yourself.

Do not settle. Be a person of character. Honor your values. Do not compromise on what is closest to your heart.

You can best help them by living with a sense of urgency. Living with purpose. Flesh out your mission.

Start small. Build on your successes. Learn from your failures. Keep moving forward. Share your story.

Bring people with you. Invite them to contribute. Give them an opportunity to risk in meaningful ways.

Identify yourself as a contributor. See yourself as a leader. Embrace a mentality of growth. Be inclusive.

Have the courage to live the life you're meant to live. Live your mission from the inside out. Shine bright so that others can see the way forward.

Chapter TwentyFive
DESTINY

"We are not human beings having a spiritual experience. We are spiritual beings having a human experience."

—*Pierre Teilhard de Chardin*

Y OU WERE CREATED to do great things with your life. Any small task can become supernatural if you pour your heart and soul into it.

You do not have to be given permission to work with all you have and apply all you know in your current circumstances.

You can choose to become your best and highest self today.

You can choose to live a life of joy, compassion and abundance.

The only person who can stop you is you, and the only person who can change you is you. You are your greatest enemy and your greatest ally.

Believe in yourself.

Unleash your full potential.

Your ability to believe in yourself directly affects your capacity to live the life you are destined for.

Your genius is tempered only by your doubt.

Your strength is held back only by your fear.

Your innate giftedness is imprisoned only by your limiting beliefs.

You already have all you need to live an abundant and remarkable life. Get out of your own way. Let go of the past. Step into your future. Start crafting a life around what really matters to you. Do the necessary things. Get to work.

Keep taking ownership. Keep being accountable to your future self. Keep living responsibly.

Structure your life around your passions. Do not be fooled. Embrace adversity. Welcome difficulty. Do hard things. Develop resilience.

Get better. Get stronger. Get smarter. Get wiser.

Acknowledge your fears, and face them.

Be disciplined. Challenge yourself every day.

Live your life. Do not copy or imitate others. Refuse to be a victim.

You have the capacity to do great things. You have the capacity to overcome the challenges in your life. You have the capacity to live with integrity. You have the capacity to persevere.

Make a conscious decision to not give up. To never quit. To never back down.

Have confidence. Learn to trust yourself. Your intuition is right 99.9% of the time. Trust your gut. Live from your soul.

Have courage. Refuse to play it safe. Follow your heart. Live with passion and determination.

Make the most of every day. Every human being has 24 hours a day. Make the most of each moment.

Let your life be good news. Be known by your compassion and your conviction. Let your actions speak. Let them speak loudly.

You are a human being, not a human doing. So be.

Stop apologizing. Start acting.

Stop blaming. Start blessing.

Stop complaining. Start creating.

Stop escaping. Start embracing.

Stop faking. Start focusing.

Stop hurting. Start healing.

Stop ignoring. Start imagining.

Stop judging. Start journeying.

Stop overcommitting. Start overcoming.

Stop pretending. Start practicing.

Stop relaxing. Start risking.

Stop talking. Start trying.

You are worth it.

A better future awaits you.

APPENDIX A
Exercises for Self-Leadership

Clarity - Why Are You Here?

Write a letter to your future self. Envision who you'll be. See your life at that specific point in the future. Make it emotional. Describe what you're doing and who you're becoming. Be specific.

Communication - What Is Your Story?

Spend 66 days writing out a daily gratitude list. Science teaches us it takes 66 days of continuous improvement to develop a new habit. Every day, write down at least 5 things you are grateful for. Keep these daily notes in your journal.

Collaboration - Who Do You Need?

Grab coffee with at least 3 people you respect and know personally. Ask them to answer the following:

- ▶ What is one thing I'm good at? Why?
- ▶ What is one area I can improve? How do you think I should go about that?
- ▶ What is one thing that has helped you improve yourself the most? Why?
- ▶ Do you have any specific advice you think I should know?

Be sure to thank them for their time.

Connection - What Is At Stake?

Buy a journal and keep track of your daily goals and commitments. Each Sunday, map out your week ahead. Spend 5 minutes writing out your personal goals for the week. Spend 5 minutes writing out your professional goals for the week. Spend 5 minutes mapping out your #1 priority for each day.

Cultivation - How Can You Help?

Examine your relationships and pick someone to invest in. Commit to meeting with that person regularly for at least 90 days. Discuss each other's goals. Challenge each other. Encourage each other. Be disciplined and consistent.

APPENDIX B
Self-Belief Assessment

Answer each of these in your journal (If you don't have one, buy one. Cheap, ruled, un-ruled, doesn't matter. The important thing is to start writing.)

The three things I am most confident about myself are . . .

Three limiting beliefs I currently have are . . .

The part of who I am I like the most is . . .

The part of who I am I like the least is . . .

My greatest personal strength is . . .

My greatest personal weakness is . . .

When I'm hungry, I usually respond by . . .

When I'm angry, I usually respond by . . .

When I'm lonely, I usually respond by . . .

When I'm tired, I usually respond by . . .

When someone is disappointed with me, I usually respond by . . .

When someone is angry with me, I usually respond
by . . .

The things I worry about the most are . . .

I feel the most excitement when I think about . . .

The one thing I feel the most positive about in life is . . .

I create the most when I . . .

What encourages me the most is in life right now is . . .

I feel most vulnerable when . . .

My greatest joy in life right now is . . .

My greatest success in life right now is . . .

I feel the most peace in life when I . . .

Someone I really admire is . . .

One thing I have always wanted is . . .

My number one goal right now is . . .

I see myself as . . .

APPENDIX C
Roadmap for Achievement

My **BIG 5 COMMITMENTS** this year are . . .

1.

2.

3.

4.

5.

My **TOP 3 VALUES** in life are:

1.

2.

3.

The **5 PEOPLE I NEED MOST** in my life are:

1.

2.

3.

4.

5.

NOTES

Chapter 4

1. Proverbs 23:7
2. Proverbs 16:18

Chapter 18

1. Luke 6:45

Chapter 23

1. Proverbs 29:18

THANK YOU

Meghan—You are the greatest gift I have received in this life.

Family and friends—Phil, Tommy, Zac, Jerrell, Vernon, James, Justin, Brent, Russ, Kevin, Matt, Brandon, Vince, Mike, and Pete (and so many others), you know who you are and how you've shaped me.

Mr. Adams—Thank you for teaching me experientially; hands down you're the best teacher I've ever had.

Casey and the team at Lucid—Thank you for helping me share this message with the world.

You—Thank you for reading this book. I wrote it for both of us.

ABOUT THE AUTHOR

Described as "a catalyst and prophetic voice," Steve teaches leaders and organizations how to discover a better way to live and work. With a passion to help people discover their innate genius, he is leading a movement to equip and inspire people to become fully alive.

Steve is the founder and lead consultant of Orbiting Normal, a global consultancy with a singular purpose—to help people discover a better way to live and work.

Steve has held a lifelong curiosity for understanding people and organizations. He specializes in helping people create a life focused on personal and professional wellbeing. He is best known for his work in the areas of leadership development, mindfulness, peak performance and self-awareness.

Through assessment, coaching and consulting, Steve has impacted 100+ organizations and 125,000+ people over the past 10 years—including Fortune 500 companies, small businesses and non-profit organizations throughout the world.

When not on the road consulting, Steve lives with his wife in Sydney's Northern Beaches.

Continue the Conversation with Steve:

steve@orbitingnormal.org
@knox_orbiting
www.orbitingnormal.org

Ready to **take your leadership to the next level?**

Join us at

THE ASYMMETRICAL LEADER RETREATS

Join Steve Knox and special guest speakers from across industries for a weekend of personal development and professional growth—3 impactful days for leaders focused on awakening the human spirit, elevating your leadership, and living your best life now.

WHAT'S INCLUDED

- One-on-one pre-retreat consulting call
- Personalized assessments and customized 360 feedback
- 10 copies of *The Asymmetrical Leader*
- A 3-year, professional goal-setting plan

ORBITINGNORMAL.ORG/EVENTS/ASYMMETRICAL-LEADER-RETREAT
Steve Knox | Lead Consultant | orbitingnormal.org | @knox_orbiting

Printed in Australia
AUOC02n1032030817
288198AU00001BA/1/P